THE CALL TO RISE

*A Guide to Healing and
Becoming the Powerful Woman
You are Meant to Be*

KELLY KRISTIN

This book is dedicated to every woman who has ever felt small, unheard, or unloved.

You are perfectly made and more powerful than you could ever imagine.

CONTENTS

INTRODUCTION

"I am going to throw you in the Hudson, and *no one is going to come looking for you*," he screamed, as my head was being slammed repeatedly into the side of the toilet in a beautiful penthouse in the highly sought-after Meatpacking district of New York City. *"No one cares about you!* They will find your body floating, and no one will even come to your funeral!"

I remember this so well. It was Christmas time. There is nothing quite like a New York City Christmas: the chill in the air, the holiday spirit, the excitement on everyone's faces. But I couldn't feel any of that. I couldn't feel anything at all.

In that exact moment, I wanted to die. I was hoping he would kill me. I thought maybe it would just all be easier, if he did throw me in that river, and I wouldn't have to live like this anymore. I wouldn't have to cry, hurt, and feel so powerless. I wouldn't have to fight anymore. I didn't feel like I had a reason to live. I didn't believe anyone cared for or loved me, and I didn't know how to love myself.

For five and a half years, that was my life.

Logically, you would think the incident I just described would have been the thing that got me to leave. You'd think I would have never stayed with anyone who could treat me that way, and you would be wrong.

It took me awhile, a few more years, but I finally did get the courage to leave. Or, rather, the Universe finally made me so uncomfortable, I no longer had a choice.

I was working as a bartender at the time in South Florida. I had just finished a seventeen-hour shift when I received a call from my then-boyfriend, as I was counting out for the night. My heart sank as soon as I heard his voice. He was drunk, incoherent, and screaming at me to tell him how to open the gate. Mind you, we had lived in the same building for over a year, so he knew how to open the gate.

I hung up, my heart racing and palms sweating. This was a familiar situation, yet something felt strangely different.

Driving home, I felt the tension within me, that sick feeling in my stomach. I was terrified, unsure of what the situation would be, and praying he would just be asleep when I got there.

And, to my surprise, he was there on the bed, incoherent, while another woman was in my bedroom.

I asked her to leave with a few choice words. Our interaction felt like a *Jerry Springer* episode, and all the while I was thinking, *Is this really my life? How did I end up here?* It was almost humorous to me, just how ridiculous I had allowed my life and home situation to become.

When she was finally gone, I began to pace. My heart was racing, I was sweating, and my fists were clenched. I went through every emotion: in and out of anger, rage, fear, and confusion. Feeling like my stomach was in my throat, I was in utter disbelief that, after all I had put up with, after everything I had been through with this man, he was now betraying me on an even deeper level.

I knew I had to go.

This was it, the last straw after I had given what seemed like an endless number of chances. This wasn't love. It had never been. I was exhausted. I had no fight left, and there was nothing to fight for.

I gathered myself and my strength and went into the bedroom to start to pack, hoping not to awaken the beast.

I got as far picking up a few random items before he woke up, calling me names and insisting I tell him what I was doing. The fight quickly escalated, and, having been in this position before, I knew what was coming.

Without thinking, I grabbed my bag and sprinted out the door. I didn't realize until I was outside that I didn't have any shoes on!

I got in my car and instantly burst into tears. My heart felt like it was exploding. I was blowing up everything I had known for so many years. I didn't know where I was going. I didn't have a plan. And I no longer cared. In that moment, all of the excuses didn't matter anymore. I promised myself that my life would never look like this again. I would never be powerless again.

###

Up until this point in my life, I had no idea of my potential, no idea of the power of my mind, body, and soul. I was operating in life from a place of accepting whatever seemed to come my way rather than from one of my own choosing. I had no idea who I was or what I was truly capable of doing and being.

This experience, although it is one I don't wish on anyone, was my wake-up call. It was my call to rise into the woman I was born to be.

I have spent my life since then in that pursuit: to be the powerful woman I was born to be and live my life in full expression. I had to find my true self. I had to find my voice, and I had to reconnect to my inner power, something I knew was within me.

If you are here, reading this, then I imagine you also feel this call. That you also feel the desire to be the powerful woman you are and the need to live life by your own design, in full expression of your truth.

I am here to tell you, no matter what you have been through, healing is possible. And when you heal, you open the door to an entirely new life.

If you desire something different for your life, it is not only possible for you. It is what you are born for. The desires in your heart are placed there for a reason. That reason is you are meant to experience those desires. You are meant to have a life that brings you joy, pleasure, and happiness.

I want you to know, whatever your circumstance and whatever your life experience has been up until this point, you, too, can break free and begin to live anew. You have more power within you than you will even know what to do with, when you learn to truly tap into it.

After being on my own healing journey for years and after helping women all across the world transform their lives from the inside out, I have created my own processes and framework to truly heal you from the root-cause trauma, emotions, stories, and beliefs that are keeping you small in life, so you can be free to live a life of your choosing.

The important thing to note is this is not a book about overcoming abuse. This is a book about overcoming all of the trauma, emotions, beliefs, and stories that hold you back from living in your full power and potential. It is about living your life in a new way that embraces and embodies your innate feminine power.

And I would like to take a second here to clarify something. When I say trauma, I am not talking purely about abuse, although that was certainly part of my experience. I am also speaking of emotional trauma, which is anything that made you feel emotionally or psychologically unsafe. If you are a human, I can bet you have experienced trauma.

Many of you may not realize all the ways unresolved trauma and harboring negative emotions can affect your life. But my hope is, by sharing my own story and insights, you can begin to heal this within yourself and create the life you are meant to be living.

I am going to share with you my rapid transformation process, so you can heal on the deepest levels possible, and can reconnect to your feminine power and internal guidance system, reprogramming your mind and body to be able to experience a new reality of your choosing.

This book will give you the roadmap I used to take myself from the most miserable and lowest point of my life to becoming a Woman Unleashed. A woman who lives life by her own rules.

A woman unleashed knows who she is, she knows what she wants, and she *gets* it. She has broken free from the patriarchal conditioning and lies that have kept her small. She dances under the moonlight. She howls to the beat of her own drum. She is connected to her innate feminine source of power. She knows her worth, and, in turn, so does everyone else.

She is magnetic, radiant and *alive*. She speaks her truth boldly with conviction and ease. She never settles and is a magnet for her desires. She doesn't give AF what others think of her. She has healed from the depths of her soul, breaking the patterns from the past. She is playful, sensual, and free. She is powerful beyond measure—a queen who knows no bounds.

We all have this potential, and yet not all of us are ready or will answer this call...

But it is truly possible for anyone who is willing to do the work.

You are and were *always* worthy of all of your heart's desires.

By following the simple steps laid out here, you will finally know how to live the life you have always wanted, in full expression, as the powerful woman have always known you are.

###

THE WAY TO RAPID TRANSFORMATION

I was elated. I was joyous. I was finally free!

From the moment I walked out that door, it was like a heavy weight I had been carrying around for years had finally been lifted. I was lighter and brighter. My usual resting bitch face became a nearly permanent smile. I started vacationing with friends, exploring my own desires, and, for the first time in as long as I could remember, I was finally doing so many things I had wanted to do for myself. I was high on life!

But while I was hoping to be able to continue to ride that wave, my body started to let me know it was not going to be so easy.

For a while, it was easy enough to ignore that my hands were shaking during moments when I would try to relax. It was easy to convince myself I was just anxious. After all, that is common now, isn't it?

It was easy to excuse my excessive drinking, my brunching for twelve hours, and my days that turned into long nights in the newfound "single life."

What became harder to ignore was the fact that I was gaining weight rapidly, about thirty pounds in three months. Or that my hair was falling out in clumps every time I brushed it. That my face had started to look foreign to me, or that I felt like a stranger in my own body, unable to sleep at night and exhausted all day. When I could sleep, I was plagued by night terrors and sleep paralysis. And to top it all off, my very regular periods just up and disappeared for months on end.

So, of course, my logical mind starting to think... *It must be my hormones.* They are just all messed up right now, but that should be a simple fix.

I went to the doctor to have myself checked out, which led to a whole slew of specialists and many tests. Eventually, I was diagnosed with PCOS (polycystic ovarian syndrome), a disease in which little cysts grow all over your ovaries in a pearl-like fashion, causing all kinds of hormonal issues. Also, my thyroid was underperforming, leaving my body with little of its own energy source, and I was told I was exhibiting signs of depression.

I have failed to mention, up until this point, that I was (and still am) a registered nurse (BSN). Yes, I know I told you I was working as a bartender. That's because, after a short, active stint, I decided I was not going to spend my life handing out pills to people and pretending that would make their health better. And to be clear, I think nurses are incredibly caring people. It is the Western medicine system and lack of a holistic understanding of the body and energy systems with which I have an issue.

That being said, when this doctor told me he was going to prescribe six different medications that I would have to be on forever, that I would never be able to have babies, and it would be incredibly hard to lose weight, that I would most likely be diabetic, and, oh, that I should go on Prozac... I kind of lost it!

I stood up and told him I would never go on any of those medications and it was preposterous that he was trying to prescribe all of this to a twenty-seven-year-old.

I was angry. I felt like the doctors were failing me. And that was when I decided to take my healing into my own hands.

I kept wondering how could a perfectly healthy young woman go downhill so fast? As I write that now, I'm laughing, but at the time, it was a very real question.

I started to read anything and everything I could about healing naturally, and I became quite obsessed with the clean lifestyle. I wanted to further my studies and also help people in the process, so I became a Holistic Health Coach at the Institute for Integrative Nutrition.

I traded Bath and Bodyworks lotions for coconut oil. I swapped out all of my chemical-laden makeup for organic. I double-filtered my drinking water and, of course, cut out all of the gluten, dairy, and sugar from my diet.

And while my gut seemed to be healing, as I was doing all the "right" things, I still wasn't fully healed. My weight would not budge, no matter how clean the diet, and I began experiencing food allergies I'd never had before. Also, my joints were hurting for no apparent reason. It became clear to me there was something much deeper going on. I wasn't going to be healed through food alone.

All of my obsessions with health and food, hormone balancing and supplements were just a distraction from a deeper truth, a truth I was running from.

My mind and body had been through immense amounts of pain, suffering, and trauma, and I was not dealing with any of that. I had two choices. I could keep going on the way I was, trying to cope with the fact of life just being this way for me, or I could go deeper and get down to what was really going on.

Logically, I could not deny the timing of these diseases and occurrences in my life. I knew I had to face the things I did not want to face. I had to feel the things I did not want to feel. And I had to take responsibility for myself on a whole new level.

This realization was not one I took lightly. We live in a society where we are conditioned to believe certain things. We are told from a young age, when you are sick, go to the doctor, and they will heal you. We are told that diseases run in the family. If we have certain genes, we will get cancer. We give our power away over and over again without questioning if it could be different.

Well, I decided to question if things could be different.

My questions led me deep into subconscious-mind work. I wanted to understand how our minds work, why we do the things we do and how to change. This led me to become a practitioner of Neuro-Linguistic

Programming (NLP), a clinical hypnotherapist and a PSYCH-K® facilitator.

I began to truly understand how to incorporate healing into our mental, emotional, spiritual, and physical bodies. And, added to my own personal studies of understanding the dynamics of embodiment and reconnection to my own feminine power, the rapid transformation process was born.

Release. Reconnect. Reprogram.

The premise is simple, and the results, profound.

While every pillar of the process will be explained in this book in depth, the overview is this:

* Release from the root cause; this means all of the trauma, emotions, beliefs, stories, and constructs that are holding you back.
* Reconnect to the truth of who you really are, your true desires, and your innate power.
* Reprogram your mind and body to be able to experience this new reality.

During my studies, I was told by numerous mentors and programs, if I just visualize and keep my attention on what I wanted to create, it would show up in my life. If I wrote my reality how I wanted it, it would begin to manifest. I was taught to keep my thoughts positive and to repeat affirmations over and over until they became true.

This is a very common practice within the personal development and coaching community, but this is where I find it truly falls flat for making transformational change in most people.

You can try to believe new things all you want. You can say all of your affirmations and have only the best intentions. Yet life doesn't change.

Why?

Because you have yet to release the things that are holding you back. You have yet to release the trauma, the beliefs, and the constructs that you have built your life upon.

What good is an affirmation, if the belief underneath it says it is not possible for you?

What good is visualizing a new reality, if your mind and body do not feel safe to experience it?

When I released from the root cause, everything changed for me. I was finally free from the past. I was finally free to be a new person.

When we have released, we are available for reconnection to our true selves and desires. Then, we are able to reprogram our mind and body to be able to achieve it.

And unlike therapy (which I find, for many people, leads to a healing cycle that can go on for years and years, but they never really feel like they are getting anywhere), this process does not leave you in the healing phase or the "let's talk about it" phase for too long. The entire premise is, when release is done (and actually still in progress, as who knows if it is ever really done?), we fill the void with a new program.

This process brings you back to a place of wholeness, while it works toward fulfilling your dreams and desires. There is nothing quite like it.

RELEASING FROM THE ROOT

Release is the first pillar in the rapid-transformation process, and for good reason. I have worked with numerous clients who are no stranger to the personal-development game. They have read all the books, taken courses, and many have even worked with other mentors, yet they did not achieve the results they were looking to. Why? Because they never got down to the root of their issues.

Much of what people (maybe even you) have done has worked through the conscious mind—saying affirmations, and journaling through emotions and feelings. Yet most of our deep-seated beliefs, values, identity, and stories—what we base our lives on—are all rooted in the subconscious (or unconscious) mind.

The latest research shows that our unconscious mind is responsible for ninety-five to ninety-nine percent of our consciousness, mind and body. Yes! Up to *ninety-nine percent*! So, basically, if you have never done this work on yourself, your life is being run completely by your unconscious programming!

Most of the time, we are either thinking about the past or worrying about the future. This leaves the present moment open to whatever programming is in your subconscious. That is why willpower is such a bad strategy for change: you are simply trying to change one behavior with another.

What *does* work? Changing on the level of identity, values, and beliefs. These are mostly all subconscious and are, thus, dictating our lives.

The unconscious mind is responsible for keeping you safe. It runs all of the complex systems of the body. (When is the last time you thought about breathing?) It also has the exact blueprint for perfect health and knows how to repair and heal. (We will speak more about this later.)

The unconscious is the domain of the emotions; it will use emotions to signal you. Have you ever experienced fear when trying a new venture? This is your unconscious mind's attempt to keep you safe. (Again, keeping you safe is its number-one job; really understanding that concept alone can change your life.) The unconscious will also organize and store your memories. This is why we interpret things based on a certain time. It will also, at times, group together certain experiences that generate the same feelings. And yes, if memories are not deemed safe to remember by your unconscious, it will also repress them and then bring them back up later, for resolution. This is actually a common occurrence during the release work.

Our unconscious is also largely programmed before the age of seven. At about that age, our brain forms what is called the "critical factor," so we are able to consciously choose if what we are told is what we want to believe. Prior to this, we take everything as our truth that we hear from those whom we believe have authority over us. That means we take on the thoughts, beliefs, and values of those who raise us, along with those of many other adult figures with whom we were in common contact.

If an older person walking down the street today decided to yell to you that you are stupid and worthless, you would probably keep on walking and shrug it off, as they are obviously crazy. But if they said that to you at five years old, you might still be acting on that, unconsciously, as your truth today.

For the longest time, I believed I was not creative. I believed I had a more logical mind. I was encouraged to go into science, and that is exactly what I did. I studied biological sciences for my first degree and then went on to become a Registered Nurse. I don't know that I ever really wanted to do or study those things. It was just what I thought I should.

I didn't value my own artistic and creative abilities. When I really started questioning this, I was able to remember exactly when I made that decision. When I was seven, an art teacher told me I should "stick to numbers." I always received poor grades in the arts, while I excelled in every other subject. In my family, the arts were also discouraged and looked on as having little value. While I longed for a creative outlet and often "wished" I was creative, I repeatedly told myself I am just not creative. I had no idea *I* was the person truly blocking myself this whole time.

However, when I started to expand my own self-awareness and capabilities, I realized I was massively creative. By letting go of that negative belief, I became able to write this book, among other things!

I could go on and on here, but the point is this. If you really want to change your life, the surface-based conscious-mind work is not going to cut it. By working in the subconscious, however, you will see faster and easier change than you ever thought possible. This work and the results that can be obtained from seemingly simple exercises and understanding continue to astonish me.

So, what do we need to release? While this may be different for everyone, certain things are true across the board. We seek to release trauma, negative emotions, and limiting decisions or beliefs that are holding you back from experiencing the life you desire.

How do you know what your current beliefs are? Take a look at your current reality. Take a look at your relationship, your financial situation, and your career. Everything you are experiencing in your outer reality is a reflection of what is going on in your inner reality.

I don't want you to just read that statement. I want you to think about it.

Go ahead now, and make an inventory of your life.

What is your current reality in these areas?

> Relationships
> Financial
> Spiritual
> Career/Business
> Physical Health
> Emotional Health

Are you happy with it? Have you attempted to change it before and not had anything stick? That doesn't surprise me. We all have a blueprint from which we operate, our baseline. If we do not choose to adjust that, we will automatically fall back into it. Do you always seem to be in a financial crisis, no matter how much money you make? How many times have you dated the exact same partner with a different face? Have you ever lost weight just to gain it all back again?

Perhaps you or someone you know always seems to have something legitimately wrong with them all of the time. This is all unconscious programming at work. And while most personal development books or strategies will tell you to change it, to work harder, to white-knuckle your way through, because you just have to reprogram your thoughts and think positively, I am here to show you a different way.

I tried the route of reprogramming. I tried to tell my body it was in perfect health, while envisioning that it was so. I tried to allow my mind to believe I was safe to be in relationships with men and imagine life with my lover. I tried to work fourteen hours a day and believe my success was inevitable.

Yet nothing really seemed to move the needle forward.

Not until I learned that the root cause of all of these issues—the root cause of relationship issues, health issues, money issues, and more—was unhealed trauma, and I could release it.

As I have explained, trauma is not just caused by physical abuse. It can be caused anytime you feel emotionally or psychologically unsafe. It is a physiological reaction in your body. Although, in my story, it is obvious I have been through much physical and emotional trauma, it is important to note there is no comparison, when it comes to trauma. There is no one who is not affected by trauma on some level. Most of us experience trauma coming into this world, during our birth. Does anyone really want to leave the warm comfort of their mother's womb and plunge into a cold world? Probably not. And thus it begins.

In addition to birth, we all experience some trauma throughout our childhood. Unfortunately, many people experience abuse, but again, that is not the only cause of trauma. Was your mom ever ten minutes late to pick you up from school? Your six-year-old brain may have gone into panic, as you thought you were being abandoned and going to have to fend for yourself. While this was not necessarily true, if you felt unsafe, you have experienced trauma.

Trauma is also passed down generationally. This is something I realized through my own self-discovery, and now, science is beginning to understand how and why.

I will discuss this idea in greater detail when I explore reconnecting with your personal power and the repression of feminine energy in our society, but here is a basic example for understanding how this works. Was your family in the Holocaust? If so, your genetic code carries the trauma your ancestors experienced.

To understand how this works, we must briefly talk about *epigenetics*. Epigenetics is influenced by your environment, what you eat, what you come into contact with on a daily basis, and how much stress you experience. It is what turns on or off gene expression. Epigenetics is the reason why one twin can end up with cancer and the other can be perfectly healthy, even though they have the exact same DNA.

Some of the trauma you are undoubtedly carrying is not even yours, yet it can be affecting how you show up in the world today and how you deal with stress and process emotions.

And at this point, you may be thinking, *"Do I have unresolved trauma that is affecting me?"*

Here are some signs that you might:

- ✓ Anger
- ✓ Fear
- ✓ Insomnia
- ✓ Addiction or substance abuse issues
- ✓ Chronic pain
- ✓ Autoimmune disorders
- ✓ Chronic infections
- ✓ Perfectionism
- ✓ Procrastination
- ✓ Lack of empathy
- ✓ Feelings of unworthiness
- ✓ Imposter syndrome
- ✓ Inability to maintain healthy relationships
- ✓ Feelings and worry about scarcity
- ✓ Personality disorders

- ✓ Depression
- ✓ Self-doubt

Quite the list, isn't it?

The good news is that awareness is half the battle. Once you are aware of something, you have the ability to change it.

And the first step to change? *RELEASE.*

Releasing will set you free.

EMOTIONAL RELEASE

As stated previously, emotions are the domain of the unconscious mind. I also like to think of them as the language of the heart.

Emotions are nothing more than energy in motion. And while that might not seem very profound, truly understanding this concept can change your life.

Just like any other form of energy, emotions can be transmuted and change form. It is also important to note that you are not your emotions. You may *have* an emotion or *feel* an emotion, but it is not *you*.

We get so accustomed to saying things like, "I am depressed," or "I am angry," when a more appropriate thing to say is, "I am having thoughts of anger."

You are not your emotions. For the most part, they are just signals. Think of it like this. When you are watching a sad movie, do you cry? Why? Nothing sad has happened to *you;* it is all happening on the screen. And you know you are watching a movie that is "make believe." Yet you can sit there with feelings of sadness. The movie has hijacked your nervous system, and you feel the emotion of being sad. You don't sit there and wonder how long it will last, though. You let it come up, and then you let it go. You are not your emotions.

Emotions are just like any other energy: in their pure state, they will just come and go. They will flow. What happens all too often, however, is we have emotions from the past that we have not dealt with. When we feel them in the present, they are compounded with all we have felt in the past.

Then, we often feel out of control and overly-emotional. We may explode with rage at something seemingly insignificant, like a car cutting us off as we drive. Or we may feel overwhelming sadness that is out of proportion to our current experience. These are all signs you have emotions that need to be released.

The reality is they are affecting your life in ways you may not even realize.

I have many clients who wonder how does this happen? Why am I like this? I used to wonder this, too.

The short answer is this. We have an event or experience that causes a feeling. This feeling causes a thought that triggers a release of chemicals in the brain. Then, the feeling intensifies, and our brain begins to associate the thought and experience with that specific feeling.

When you experience that same feeling again (after something totally different than the original experience), a compounded effect is created. Now, this is all fine and good, if they are positive or desirable emotions. (For example, I thank Goddess I get to experience compounded joy on the regular!). But it is not so good, if the emotions are negative, like anger or sadness.

Releasing from the root-cause experience of this emotion (the first time it ever occurred in your unconscious memory) will change the association the brain has with that feeling, and thus will change your perception and experience of that feeling going forward.

Some of these root emotions are in our past life. Some are passed down generationally. In nearly all cases, they happened before the age of seven years old. As I explained earlier, the unconscious mind is largely imprinted before the age of seven. This is the time when most of our values, beliefs, and identity are formed.

If you are wondering how our unconscious mind can remember a past life, there is no need to worry. You do not need to believe in past lives for this to work. Your beliefs are your own, and I am not here to debate them. Just know that the unconscious mind is highly metaphorical and will give you the exact image and message you need to know, in order to be able to let go of that emotion from the root.

Can you imagine no longer getting triggered by anger? No longer walking around feeling the fear, sadness, guilt, or shame you have grown accustomed to?

One of my clients was dealing with some difficulty in her relationship with her mother. Now, she was not new to personal development or spiritual growth. She had done much of her own work, but she just felt she was not able to let go of the tension she experienced in their relationship and the underlying distrust she had of her mother.

After our initial interview, I released with her the root emotions of anger, fear, sadness, and guilt. To her surprise, a majority of these emotions were rooted in past lives. By releasing them in the past, we were actually able to change her in the present. She instantly reported feeling differently toward herself and her mother.

Once these root emotions are released, we can then work on specific scenarios and limiting decisions relative to the situation. In this particular client's case, I asked her unconscious to bring about the scenario that would result in her letting go the distrust of her mother. What came up?

An image of her parents fighting when she was three years old. She did not have any conscious recollection of this. But after releasing the trauma around that event and bringing her back to the moment of now, everything shifted. In our follow-up months later, she reported having a completely different relationship with her mother. Her body no longer got tense near her, and they no longer fight.

Was her mother any different? No.

But by changing herself, her perceptions, and her reactions, she has changed the world and the relationships around her.

This was all done in a one-day intensive with minimal follow-up. Now, of course, everyone is different, and some people need more intensive work than others, based on their personal experiences, histories, and willingness to let things go.

Take for instance my client, Dan. He came to me wanting to really change his life. He was stuck in a rut with his business, had not had a significant relationship for years, and was depressed about his position in life, overall. He came to me for my work in subconscious reprogramming and its ability to clear trauma, as he felt there were some events in his past that were really holding him back.

Dan was an interesting case. I knew he had what he felt was a deep, dark secret tearing him up inside. He was living in this event, unable to speak about it. He felt like it was weighing him down, and he was not able to be himself. And although he sought me out, he was also highly skeptical of the work and processes. (Sometimes, it feels too easy to actually be working!)

We worked through his resistance, and after a couple of months, we were able to release enough blockages and root emotions that we were able to work through this particular event. Once the subconscious let us know we were safe to proceed, we were able to do a PSYCH-K® process to change the perception and resolve the trauma.

This led to an almost instantaneous healing. Dan was finally able to release the shame and guilt he had been carrying. From that moment on, he was a different man. As a result of this, he was able to rebuild relationships in his family that had been nearly destroyed by this event and the subsequent years of his holding on to it.

He now reports an overall excitement and vigor for life. Also, he is in a lovely relationship with a person he feels is his soul mate.

TRUE HEALING IS MIND AND BODY

For most of us, at some point while we were growing up, we learned it was either wrong or bad to show all of our emotions. We learned it was not safe to express ourselves authentically, and thus we built up coping mechanisms to deal with it. You may have been told to "stop crying" in the middle of a pure emotional expression or "get over it" when you wanted to fully express. Maybe you were forced to be a good little girl and make sure you played nicely, which meant you were not allowed to express what was truly going on inside of you.

Quite simply, we are never taught how to process our emotions. And while releasing the emotions from their root will certainly help us alleviate some of the coping mechanisms and repair the damage that holding on to emotions has done, we must also become aware of the patterns we have developed to keep us safe and loved in this world, along with all of the ways we learned to not feel our emotions.

One of the most common ways to not feel our emotions is to live outside of our body. And while, yes, you are certainly experiencing life with your body right now, you may not truly be embodying it.

Common ways we leave our body are through overeating, using alcohol or drugs, endless scrolling on social media, overspending, Netflix binging, and excessive sex or masturbation.

Now, I am not here to say you can never watch a show on Netflix or pleasure yourself (I am *all* about self-pleasure). But is that your go-to, when you are upset? Do you feel compelled to this behavior, so it's not like you are choosing it? Is eating a carton of ice cream your way of dealing with your anger? Do you watch an episode or an entire season?

For me, it was a mixture of many of the above. One that became particularly apparent and nasty was binge-eating. What is most interesting about it is, at the time when I was knee-deep in holistic health studies and knew everything I was "supposed" to do and eat, to be healthy, my binging and, often, purging were at their worst.

As embarrassed as I am to admit this, I actually looked forward to my binges. There was something really satisfying about shoving excessive amounts of food in my face. I would be almost giddy on shopping day, as I would fill my cart with all the things I would inhale within moments of purchasing them. Oftentimes, I wouldn't even wait until I got home. I would eat it all in my car and then be upset I didn't have more. There were even times when I would binge and purge multiple times throughout the same day.

Consciously, I would tell myself I had to stop, that I was killing myself. I would promise this was the last time, and yet I could not stop. I felt like someone else had taken over my body. No matter how much I tried to talk myself out of it, I would soon find myself again inhaling all the food I could get my hands on.

What I did not know or recognize at the time was this was just another way for me to avoid dealing with the trauma I had been through. It was my way of controlling things at a time when being inside my body felt very unsafe and out of control. By feeling the fullness of food and the pleasure and endorphins from taking in massive amounts of sugar, I did not have to experience the discomfort of what was happening underneath.

While I went to the extreme with my bingeing, I cannot think of a single woman with whom I have ever worked who did not have some issues around food. Whether it was bingeing, starving, obsessing about calories, endless dieting, or eating too many candies, it is all one in the same. And if that is you, the question to ask yourself is this: what are you really hungry for? What does your body truly desire? This is something to ponder now. We will expand more on this in my section on reconnection.

So, if the answer is not to try and run away from or stuff down our emotions, what do we do instead?

Feel it. Feel the emotion as it comes up. Do not judge it or try to make it wrong. Notice it and let it go.

And while this may be easier said than done, I will share with you some powerful practices to process emotions as they come up. This is incredibly important, because anytime we are not in the moment, feeling what we are being asked to feel and processing the emotions, we can cause that emotion to get stuck. Stuck emotions cause underlying stress and inflammation in your body that can manifest as disease, such as chronic pain or, in my case, autoimmune and eating disorders.

Release the emotion, and you can relieve the pain and heal. I am proud to say I no longer suffer from any autoimmune conditions and no longer struggle with my food. In fact, I now eat a diet consisting of entirely what I truly desire to eat, and I find joy in each bite. Doing my own trauma and emotional release work has allowed me to release all of my excess weight. I no longer worry about what foods I should or shouldn't be eating. I let my body and intuition guide me, and I have given up my obsession with getting it perfect. This has been one of the biggest gifts clearing trauma has given me.

Stuck emotions can also show up in different ways, and you may believe they have a legitimate reason to be there; for example, after an injury in your body.

For years, on and off, I had a pain in the middle of my back. Initially, this was caused by a car accident that led to a dislocated rib head. But that is not the whole picture!

This specific pain would come up in certain periods of my life for what I thought was "no reason." There was no physical trigger, and for a while, I thought I was going to have to experience this pain for the rest of my life. It was not until I began to realize, through continuing to raise my own level of self-awareness, that this pain would come up when I was telling myself the story that I was unsupported.

For example, when I was moving and I expected help from a few friends who didn't show up, my back flared up in pain. I knew I hadn't done anything to physically cause this, although I was under quite a bit of stress. When I tuned in to how I was really feeling, the word "unsupported" came up. This made total sense! My rib head, which is connected to my spine (the literal support system of the body) was experiencing pain when I felt lacking in support.

Now, feeling unsupported was a story that began a long time ago. It showed up during my childhood and it continued to show up in my life, until recently.

I asked my unconscious mind to take me back to the first time when I felt unsupported. To my surprise, I was taken to an image of me tending to a fire *four lives ago*! I was panicking, because the fire was going out, and it was my job to keep it burning. I was trying everything to keep it burning, but it went out.

I asked my unconscious what I needed to learn, to let this go. The answer? *ASK*. Ask for help. It is not that I was being unsupported, per se. It was that I needed to *ask for help,* because, really, I am always being supported.

This realization was profound. I also recognized a theme in my life, when I did not ask for help even when I desperately needed it.

Case in point: the abusive relationship. Why did I not ask anyone for help? Why did I not tell my parents, or friends or anyone? Because I was afraid to ask for help. I grew up believing, if I made my own bed, I had to lie in it. This, of course, was something I was told throughout my childhood, but the roots of it clearly go back much further.

I took this answer and proceeded to do a ritual. I did some light breath work, created a sacred space for myself, and then asked for support. I asked to feel the support of Mother Earth below me and all of the realms of magic that I cannot see.

I let myself be held by the Earth. I let myself feel what needed to be felt. I cried. I cried so hard, I could barely breathe. I didn't really know what I was even crying for—it just wanted to come out. So I cried until I didn't want to cry anymore.

The results? I woke up with a perfectly functioning, pain-free back that, the day before, had been in such excruciating pain, I could barely move. And I have not experienced any pain at that spot in my back since doing that work.

Now, while it may be easy to think this could have been some kind of fluke or anomaly, I can confirm I have had similar results with my clients.

Take, for instance, my client Maria. She and I were working together in one of my one-on-one program intensives. During one of our sessions, she complained of shoulder pain. She was very upset that she had hurt her shoulder, as it was messing with her workouts and other things she wanted to do.

I asked her when it started hurting and, with her permission, tapped into her subconscious, to see the underlying reason for the pain. The answer? A feeling of resentment she was carrying toward her husband. We resolved the negative feeling, and, by the end of our one-hour session, she was moving her shoulder pain-free.

While you may never be perfectly present to every emotion and story in your life, it is important to check in with yourself on what your current way of dealing with it is. If you get angry now, do you allow yourself to feel it? If you are sad, do you allow yourself to cry? Or do you instantly start to tell yourself you are wrong or bad for feeling these emotions and then attempt any way possible to feel better?

Do you allow yourself to feel negative emotions? Or do you try to shove them down through self-sabotaging behavior? In what ways do you leave your body?

If you have been unaware to doing this in the past, recognize it may take some time. This is part of reconditioning yourself as the powerful and sovereign woman you are.

When you feel an emotion arise, instead of trying to push it away, turn toward it. Ask yourself, "What is this about?" And ask this from a place of curiosity, not judgment. When you ask, you are letting your nervous system know this is not a threat, this is just something to explore. You understand that this is arising in you as a signal from your body. So, what is your body trying to tell you?

Do not resist the emotion. Let it sit there, feel it, and then let it go. Continue to separate yourself from the emotion, and become the observer of your thoughts. If the emotion persists, you are most likely thinking thoughts that are keeping the feeling there.

If you are having trouble letting the emotion go, you can process it through your body, instead of letting it build up. Do you feel anger? Start having temper tantrums now. Sad? Cry. And stop deciding whether any emotions are good or bad. Is it more comfortable to be happy rather than angry? Maybe.

Personally, I have come to enjoy getting angry. It reminds me I am human and have feelings. It was never safe for me to express my anger growing up, but now, it feels freeing.

For me, anger is processed by my putting on some rock music. My favorite are either Smashing Pumpkins' "Bullet with Butterfly Wings" or Rage Against the Machine's "Killing in the Name of." Then

I let it all out. I run around my house, throwing and punching pillows, screaming and seething and acting like an all-out crazy person.

I am sure, if anyone were to observe me doing this without context, they would think I had lost my mind. And I am perfectly okay with that.

If I am feeling sad, there is nothing like some old-school Mariah Carey for me. I let the words flow into my heart. I feel the pain, I see it, I observe, I love it, and I tell it is all already all right. I move my body, and then it is gone. This is not done in the moment, per se. However, it is part of my regular practice to move my body with the intention of letting emotions out.

The gym is also a favorite place for me to process emotions. I have never met an emotion that a good boxing class could not break through.

I suggest you also find a practice or creative outlet for your emotions. Perhaps it is going for a walk or a run. Maybe it is creating art or journaling. Whatever it is, make sure you do it regularly. This is putting yourself and your health first.

For most people, the work of releasing does not stop with just emotions. We must go further to release the stories, beliefs, and past identities we are holding onto that are not serving us, either.

RELEASING PAST IDENTITIES

"When I let go of who I am, I become what I might be."

~*Lau Tzu*

While it may sound simple to release, I want you to know you will most likely feel resistance to doing this work. It is often uncomfortable to look at yourself objectively and see all the places where you have been the person holding yourself back.

Oftentimes, when we go back to the root issues as adults, we find they now seem insignificant, which can cause self-judgment and ridicule. It is important to understand, to you as a child, those feelings were very real and now need to be validated. The point is to not stay there. It is to look at these wounds and emotions and stories in order to let them go. Then, you are free to create a story and a life of your own choosing.

Everything is a story, and the story you tell yourself about yourself is what will determine your reality, because it is tied in so deeply with your subconscious identity. Your identity is the deepest layer of your unconscious and determines so much of your life. You simply cannot be who you are not.

Now, I want you to pause for a second. Are you making up a story in your head about the fact that I just told you everything is a story? It is key that you understand this important point, in order to make a significant transformation in your life.

- ➢ What is the story you tell yourself about yourself?
- ➢ Is life easy or hard for you?
- ➢ Have your experiences been here to serve you or to harm you?
- ➢ Do people always let you down, or are you being supported?
- ➢ Is making money easy or hard?
- ➢ Are you hard or easy to love?

➤ Are you confident or shy?

➤ An introvert or an extrovert?

These stories grow out of your experiences and the ways you interpret them, based on your underlying unconscious beliefs. If you believe you are hard to love, you will continue to manifest experiences that validate that belief and reinforce the story. If you continue to tell the story that you are shy and not confident, you will continue to be that way. This is how the subconscious mind works. It wants to please you and make sure you are always right.

Also, you are never really seeing the whole picture consciously. The amount of data our unconscious mind takes in is much greater than what we can process consciously. When you believe something, you will see it, because you have directed your unconscious mind to look for it, as something you want. It is incredibly important that you understand this point. You see what you believe. When you change your beliefs, the things that you see will change, too. They were always there, but now you are now able to see and process things differently, because *you* are different.

You always have a choice about what you make things mean. Nothing has any meaning except for whatever meaning you give it, and so much of your personal power lies in the meaning you give to experiences and circumstances in your life. Change your stories and beliefs about yourself, and you will change your life.

You are not what happened to you. You are not a diagnosis. And all too often, I see people trying desperately to hang onto these stories and experiences and aspects of identity, because they fear being lost without them.

Your story is your own. Yes, things have happened, maybe even bad things, maybe terrible and traumatic, but it is how you choose to interpret the experience that dictates your reality. When you realize this, and truly understand the stories you tell yourself can be changed, you will open up yourself to a whole new world. The world where you choose. You choose who you get to be and how life gets to go for you.

We often wonder, *if I let this go, then who will I be?* And that is precisely where the breakthrough occurs: in the unknown. When you let go of who you have been, you can become who you are truly meant to be. Who you are meant to be is simply who you desire to be.

Your wounds and experiences were not meant to hold you down and keep you small. They are merely experiences that are here to serve you and propel you to the next level in your soul's progression. It is a failure to understand this that holds people back.

Who are you without your story?

One of my favorite things is when a client says to me, "I just feel like I don't even know who I am anymore."

My usual response is, "Did you ever?"

I'd like you to think about this for a moment: do you know who you are?

Do you know what it is that makes you do the things you do? What makes you like the things you like? This life you are living, have you chosen it? Or did it just all seem to happen?

And if you are starting to get the feeling that maybe you don't know who you are, that is okay. The adventure begins when you decide you are worth finding.

Think of this moment as a new adventure, where you are an explorer and observer to your own experience. Be willing to see and experience things in a new way. Release the need to hold on to anything being a certain way for you, and open up to the possibility of life being better than you ever thought it could be. You are the kind of person who life works out for. Everything is working in your favor all of the time. You get to decide to change the story any time you want.

RELEASING GENERATIONAL TRAUMA

"Every woman who heals herself helps heal all women who came before her and all those who come after her."

~Christiane Northrup

Trauma can be passed down from one generation to the next. In the simplest context, whatever happened to your mother was passed on to you, and what she experienced was passed to her through her own mother, literally carried in your genetic code. This is a simple concept to understand, but it can quickly become complex when we start to bring all women into the conversation.

If you are a woman living in today's patriarchal society, I guarantee you that you are being affected by the oppression of the feminine.

If you recall, part of my body's breaking down was when I developed PCOS, an autoimmune disorder that results in unbalanced sex hormones, which causes little cysts to form on top of the ovaries. After learning about the things I have laid out in this book so far, it was no surprise to me that my body reacted in this way. We women hold a lot of trauma and pain in our womb space (this houses the uterus and ovaries). I am proud to say, though, that I no longer show any signs or symptoms of PCOS, and I take no medication for it. I resolved the trauma, and my body followed suit.

While it may be easy to say that my particular PCOS could have been caused by the abusive relationship I was in, that is never the whole story.

In our society, PCOS is very common, along with endometriosis, hormone imbalances, infertility, and other issues affecting the womb space. These conditions are affecting women at an alarming rate. While some of this can be blamed on living in a chemical-laden society, with a food system filled with modified ingredients, which has led to overall poor health for our population, there may be a deeper cause underneath this situation. Recently, a nervous system connection was found between the brain and the uterus directly. To me, this had profound implications. Knowing this now, it makes perfect sense that women are experiencing so much disease and issues having to do with the womb space.

Women are under an almost constant low-lying stress or heightened awareness in daily life. I know, for myself, there are places I will not go alone, I may go a different direction, instead of walking into a group that could potentially be threatening. No, I am not paranoid. This is just being a smart woman who has had to deal with catcalling, harassment, and much more for basically my whole life. And I know many other women who feel the same way. Perhaps you are one of them.

But have you ever wondered how this hyper-vigilance affects you?

We know that stress causes inflammation, and inflammation is the root of all disease. And since your brain, which perceives the stress, is directly connected to your uterus, this explains why so many women are struggling with hormones imbalances, PCOS, endo, fertility issues, and more. It is simply trauma at work again! This is not just a personal issue. It is a collective issue.

The uterus is not the only place where women seem to be experiencing an uptick in dysfunction. Consider this fact: women are five- to eight-times more likely to experience thyroid issues than men are. (I was one of them.) If the cause was just the poor food and chemicals we are bombarded with, living in our modern society, wouldn't the rates between men and women be more similar?

Have you ever considered how the thyroid gland is located at the center of the throat chakra, which often gets blocked when one is not speaking their truth? In my case, it was easy to blame my thyroid issues on the fact that my voice was suppressed during my toxic relationship, when I had to constantly watch what I said, leaving me in constant fear of saying the wrong thing and triggering a blowout.

After developing greater self-awareness and doing this healing work, I saw how this suppression actually started in my childhood, when I began to learn it was not safe for me to process or express emotions. And it goes even beyond that. You see, I am not the only person in my family to experience thyroid issues. My mother, my sister, and even her children all have issues with their thyroid. So, what is really going on here?

For centuries now, women have lived in a patriarchal society. We are seen as the lesser sex, the weaker sex. It was not all that long ago when women who spoke their truth and stood up for themselves were called witches and burned at the stake. In fact, just a few hundred years ago, I, too, would have been burned for writing and speaking about the things I do.

I am quite sure, somewhere in your ancestry, you have a woman who had to keep quiet to stay alive. And as I mentioned earlier, these traumas are passed down in your genetic code, so they continue to affect you today. By your choosing to do this work, however, and choosing to release this generational trauma, you are transforming not just yourself, but the past and the future for every woman. I truly commend you for your bravery.

Patriarchal conditioning runs deep within our culture. We are cyclical beings who work in a masculine-structured society. We learn at a young age that we must hold our emotions and feelings inside, in order to be successful. We learn that what we feel doesn't necessarily matter and that we must ignore our bodies and just keep pushing through, keep going to work, and keep on keeping on.

Women have traditionally been in caregiver roles. They continue to wildly outnumber men in caregiving jobs such as nursing. Do you think this is a coincidence? No. This is all part of our patriarchal conditioning. This is also a big reason why women often get stuck in the people-pleasing cycle.

We have been conditioned to believe our worth is somehow tied up in what we are doing for and giving to others. While it is certainly a nice notion to be giving and loving, it becomes detrimental when you please others over your own needs, when you say yes but you desperately want to say no. Or when you are always the last person on your list.

This creates a relationship with self that is rooted in self-betrayal. When you feel that you cannot trust yourself, you are in your head instead of in your body. You doubt your intuition, and you lose the ability to connect with your true self.

As you wake up to this conditioning and see all of the ways it is not serving you, and then you choose to release these ideas and the things you think you "know" about how the world works, you will now be free to reconnect to your core, to your body, and to your feminine power, and you'll be able to recondition yourself to live in your own truth.

RECONNECT TO YOUR TRUTH

Who are you?

You are not your emotions. You are not your thoughts. You are not the things that have happened in your life. So, then, who are you?

We could stop this whole thing right now, if we all just understood this. You are a limitless cosmic being having a human experience.

You are here for your soul's growth and progression. This life is not meant to keep you down. You are not here to suffer, to struggle, or to be consumed by your fears or doubts of not being enough. In fact, your fears are like signals showing you the direction you should go and what things you are here to create. Without fear being present, you would not know the way to go. You can no longer let these things stop you from expressing and being who you truly are.

You are here to experience everything this life has to offer. You are here to live in abundance, joy, and love. All of those things you thought made you wrong or bad—what if they were your calling? What if they were your greatest strengths? What if all you had to do was decide what you want out of this life, in order to create it?

What is it that you really want?

What is your soul begging you and guiding you toward that you just keep ignoring?

If you are like most people I have worked with and encountered, the answer is:

"I don't know what I want"

This is a phrase I have heard more times than I can count. So many women have spent their lives in a way that is all about pleasing others and making themselves lovable in the eyes of another. When you do this throughout your life, it becomes almost impossible to truly know what you want. You have been walking around disconnected from your truth, from your power, and from your body for so long, the question "what do you want?" is terrifying.

And it is also the most important question you may ever ask yourself.

To be frank, healing and releasing are completely wasted, if you do not continue on with these next steps in the process. While you may have much more awareness as to why you are the way you are and can now recognize the patterns while feeling less triggered, after doing the release work, it is still a program you can go back to, if you do not decide to do something else with yourself.

When you release, it is like you are creating a vacuum of empty space in your mental, emotional, spiritual, and physical bodies. The Universe does not like vacuums, so it will fill it with something. If you just release and give your mind nothing else to fill in the space, you will have no choice but to go back to the old patterns and ways of being and thinking. This sets you up for a never-ending cycle of healing. You will discover that a new thing you have to deal with always seems to pop up.

Knowing what you want is imperative. Vision is imperative. When you have a vision for yourself and your life, you have a direction you can go in. This is massively important, first as a motivating factor: knowing what you are working toward can get you to actually do the work and take the steps required. Second, having a vision is important for your mind. As I mentioned before, your unconscious mind wants to please you. It wants to help you. When you let it know what you want, it will use the filters to alert you to the right path in order to attain it.

I want you to think now:

➢ Do you currently have or do anything you actually want to?

➢ Have you chosen the life you are living?

➢ Or is it filled with a bunch of things you think you must do?

➢ How about your job and relationship? Did you choose them? Or did you just fall into and accept what came along?

This is often the first thing I ask my clients: What do you want?

The answers are often:

> "I don't want to feel this way anymore."
> "I just want to be happy."
> "I want to live a good life."

The issues here are, if you are focusing on what you *do not* want, you are not focusing on what you *do* want. Quite simply, you are where your attention and focus is.

Your subconscious mind does not process the word "not." So, whenever you say something like, "I don't want to feel this way anymore," your mind interprets that to mean, "I want to feel this way."

This will give you a better picture. If I told you, "Do *not* think of a gold statue," I can guarantee an image of a gold statue just popped into your mind. The image must arise in order for you to "not" think about it... Thus, you are thinking about it! I hope this helps you start to see just how powerful your mind is and why your language and thoughts are so very important.

To say something like, "I don't know what I want," is also flat-out false. You *do* know, because true desire comes from your soul, and your soul always knows.

You have desires planted into your heart. They come to you in dreams, in visions, and in the "I wish I could do *that*" rhetoric. Most of the time, you just shut these down and tell yourself they could never happen for you or that you are crazy.

You have been conditioned to give up on your dreams in pursuit of a life you never really wanted to live. You allowed society to tell you it was wrong or bad to want the things that you truly want. Or perhaps you fell into the spiritual myth of living a simplistic and non-materialistic lifestyle, as a higher way of being.

Let us clear this up once and for all. If you desire something, it is because you are meant to experience it. If you are at all familiar with quantum theory, you actually already do have the things that you desire.

I will break this down further. In the quantum, there is absolutely no time or space, which means there is no past or future, either. There is only the moment of now, and everything is occurring all at once. This is the field of pure potentiality, which means everything you desire is a potential for you, a potential that, should you choose to align with it vibrationally, it will become available to you.

If this is the first time you have heard this concept, please read that again and know that we will be revisiting this topic again, in the reprogram section.

For now, it is enough to know that the desires in your heart are meant for you. Before you can have them, you have to know how to hear them, see them, and feel them. You have to learn how to reconnect to your body, so you can hear your intuition and your internal guidance system.

Intuition is the voice, the whisper, the nudge that is guiding you from within. The only way to hear it is to be in silence and tune in. The easiest way to do that is through meditation. When you meditate and become the observer of your thoughts, feelings, and emotions, you are separating yourself from them. You are reconnecting to your core and the truth of who you really are as a limitless being.

Meditation, or really any practice that allows you to get out of your head, will aide you as we next begin to reconnect to your truths. And the first place to start this reconnection process is the very place where we had to release so much: Childhood.

RECONNECT TO YOUR INNER CHILD

What is the inner child? Quite literally, it is the child who lives within you. It is the part of you that still retains its innocence, a quest for joy, and a sense of awe and wonder about the world.

When you lose touch with this aspect of self, you lose your joy and your sense of exploration and freedom. Instead, you walk around taking yourself and life so seriously, you forget that beauty is all around you and this life is truly magical.

When is the last time that you expressed pure uninhibited joy? When is the last time you followed that joy to take you somewhere or do something, perhaps even something that you were not "supposed" to do?

Regardless of your relationship with yourself and with joy, your inner child has never left you. Oftentimes, she is there, waiting for you to love her, to pay attention to her, and to console and forgive her for the things you may have blamed her for. To tell her it is not her fault and she was doing the best she could. This allows for positive integration of your inner child into who you are now.

Think about the beautiful attributes we carry as children. We have no fear; we fall down and just keep getting back up again. We laugh at novelty and are curious about the world around us. We love everyone. We don't question if we are worthy of having or doing something. These are the attributes that, as adults, we can tend to leave behind; and instead, we have a wounded child running our life.

Many of us were not parented in a way that made us feel loved, worthy, and nourished. And this is not a statement of blame, as I understand and believe, people can only give what they know and have. I also hold the firm belief that everyone is doing the best they can with their own personal circumstances and experiences. This is a belief I highly suggest you integrate into your own life. It allows you to forgive others and yourself.

Choosing to forgive your parents or anyone who raised you sets you free. It also puts you into a position of empowerment through the realization that you now get to parent yourself. This is about taking responsibility for yourself and your life. You get to take care of yourself in the ways you wish you had been all along. You are the one, now, who gets to meet the needs of this inner child within you.

And that is the work, as you reparent yourself now. This is about accepting and loving all parts of yourself and giving yourself what you truly need to feel nourished and loved.

I would like you to think of a child, perhaps two years old. Would you say the things to them that you currently say to yourself? Would you blame them, tell them they are stupid or less than others, because of how they look, their weight, or what they choose to do with themselves?

Or would you encourage them? Love them? Tell them they are doing the best they can?

Connecting back to your inner child is about learning trust and forgiveness. What do you need to forgive your inner child for? Where have you been pushing her away and, in turn, denying yourself joy?

Think about all the things you used to do as a child. What did you enjoy? What did you love doing for hours and hours? Was it drawing? Painting? Dancing? Playing outside? Grabbing a pretend microphone and singing?

If you are having a hard time thinking of anything, that is okay. Perhaps you'll have a memory come up where you were just laughing—it is pure joy. I want you to take that and carry it forward with you.

Once you reconnect to this aspect within yourself, find ways to actively express it. Seek out new experiences that bring your inner child joy. Go out with the pure intention of being playful and silly. The more you do this, the more this child within you will feel safe to be there and help you experience more joy in your life. Joy is massively healing and also one of the most powerful vibrations you can put out into the universe. The more joy you emit, the more comes back to you.

Healing this aspect within yourself also requires doing the self-care necessary to meet your needs. Checking in with yourself and asking what you need to feel good should become a regular practice. Perhaps it is going for a walk out in nature. Maybe it is getting a massage. It could be saying no to something you don't actually want to do, when you would have otherwise said yes just to please someone else. People-pleasing is often the sign of a childhood wound that started with the belief that you must be doing something for others in order to receive love.

To truly move on from this wound, you must develop habits that serve you. Habits of discipline with yourself. Do you do the things for yourself that you say you will? This is self-integrity, and it is incredibly healing, as well as a quality that will move you forward in this life.

I recommend you start small. What is one thing you can commit to doing today? Perhaps it is a five-minute meditation. Maybe it's reading a few pages in a new book. It doesn't matter what it is. It just matters that you do whatever you say you will. When you keep your word to yourself, you reinforce to your mind that you are worthy of change and worthy of receiving what it is that you desire.

Just like a child is worthy for no reason at all, so are you. You are worthy just because you are. It is time to start approaching your life that way.

It is time to start experiencing the joy, love, and beauty that is all around you. Tell your inner child she is safe to come back home, that you are there to take care of her and love her.

And with your inner child with you now, it is time to embrace your feminine power.

RECONNECT TO YOUR FEMININE POWER

I'm a woman
Phenomenally.
Phenomenal woman,
That's me.

~Maya Angelou

What does it mean to be a woman?

This is a question I have pondered throughout my self-awareness and healing journey. While we are told the obvious differences between men and women, such as we have different "private parts," and the stereotypes, like women are more emotional than men, this has never felt satisfying. I never felt these descriptions and distinctions really gave me the answer I was looking for.

THE CALL TO RISE

What does it mean to be a woman? Does it mean you are a natural-born caregiver? Does it mean you must be polite and "lady-like"? Or perhaps be a "good girl" and just sit down, shut up, and look pretty?

Does it mean you must be soft? Does it mean you are weak? What does it mean to be a woman?

Have you ever had the thought that it would just be easier to be a man? Men sure don't have to worry about emotions and periods and being lusted after. They're not seen as sexual objects who exist only for a man's pleasure, either. Are you tired of feeling like a second-class citizen in a society that is clearly set up for men?

I had all of those thoughts before I truly understood my own power and magic, before I understood what it meant to be a woman. I am still on this journey, awakening more and more every day to this truth, to this innate power within me, and it is the gift that just keeps on giving.

Women are the most powerful beings on the planet. We are creators of life, portals to the other side.

We are divinity in human form. It is time now to embody your fullness as a woman. When fully embodied, there is no limit to what you can create. There is no limit to your abilities to manifest. You are more powerful and magical than you could ever imagine. The key to tapping into this divinity is by connecting to and embracing your feminine power.

You see, for centuries, women were considered the wise ones. They were respected, revered, and honored. Ancient civilizations honored the divine feminine through prayer, rituals, and dance. However, somewhere between the onset of agriculture and structured religion, the patriarchy was born. And with it, we started to lose the magic of being a woman.

Fast forward to our current culture. It is clear the masculine energy is thriving and feminine embodiment has had to suffer. Now, when I say "masculine" and "feminine," I am not just speaking about men and women. I am referring to the energies that exist within all of us. Masculine energy is logical and linear; it is rooted in realism and structure. Masculine energy is more focused on doing and achieving. Think of the common corporate structure: you have timelines and goals and things that must be done. The feminine is more about being and presence to the moment. It is not linear or logical, and that is one of the greatest strengths, giving those tapped into their feminine power the ability to make massive change in short amounts of time. Feminine energy is rooted in intuition, creativity, and flow.

To break it down in simplest terms, masculine energy is in the head, and feminine energy is in the body. As women, in order to be truly powerful, we must connect to our bodies. Now, of course, the goal is not *only* to be in our feminine, since a lack of balance can bring about its own issues. But I have found most women are truly disconnected from their feminine energy, and if they are more feminine, it is wounded rather than empowered (a topic we will discuss shortly).

We live in a very masculine, driven society. Women are working nine-to-five jobs, eating the same foods every single day, doing the same routine daily, and walking around completely disconnected from their bodies. We live in our heads instead of in our hearts. Many of us are overeating, overworking, binge watching on Netflix, and endlessly scrolling on social media. This lack of feminine energy is a true problem in many of the woman I have coached. How does this show up?

> In pushing so hard to constantly do, do, do.
> In pretending like everything is "fine," when you feel like you are falling apart on the inside.
> In being afraid to ask for help and support out of fear you'll be labeled "needy."
> In ignoring your body and all the signals she sends to you.
> In saying *YES* when you want to say *NO*.
> In feeling like you can't express your emotions or have to stuff them down to be accepted.

Here is some more evidence of a lack of the feminine in our lives:

> Sex feels like a chore or something to check off the list.

- ➢ You are obsessed with systems and strategy and thinking your way through things; everything is "logical."
- ➢ You are constantly in the "hustle," afraid to slow down and just be.
- ➢ You don't consider your own pleasure and your own joy, and you are much more keen to do for others.
- ➢ You don't even *allow* yourself to feel the joy and pleasure, because you fear it won't last, so what exactly is the point?
- ➢ You may have autoimmune disorders or you may hold onto weight you just can't seem to "lose" or you seem to have other "mysterious" health issues.
- ➢ You feel like you have to *try* so damn hard at everything; that you could only ever be successful from "hard work."
- ➢ Even though you may be financially successful and/or have that killer career or business that so many women long for, you feel unfulfilled and like a piece of you is missing.

➢ Your relationship (if you have been able to maintain one) is out of balance; you don't feel loved or understood like you want to be.

➢ You have lost your magnetism and your lust for life.

➢ You are tired, emotionally and physically, and you feel spiritually disconnected.

➢ You have lost true expression of yourself.

I *know,* because I have experienced nearly all of these things. I had no idea how disconnected I was from myself, my body, and my intuition for the majority of my life. I also had no idea just how healing it would be to reconnect to my feminine power.

The Catch? Feminine embodiment and truly tapping into your feminine power is a difficult thing for many women to attain. For so long, we have been conditioned to be quiet and not to show our emotions. We have been shamed for being sexual, sensual, and who we really are.

Being in your feminine energy is a highly vulnerable state for anyone. And being vulnerable is not a safe place to be, for your nervous system. The nervous system reaction is what typically keeps many women away from embodiment and truly feeling what needs to be felt. If you have been shut-down emotionally, it will take you some training to get there, but it is worth it.

After leaving my abusive relationship, I went through a period of time when I was constantly "on." I would work long hours and pick up extra shifts at the bar. At this time, I was also selling medical devices and taking my courses to become a certified health coach, while I had started my own drop-shipping ecommerce store.

I was also consuming massive amounts of information, between books, audios, and podcasts. I would even put on audio recordings while I was taking a shower. I could not stand to be in silence. I could not stand to be in my own thoughts. And, instead of processing and being, I was constantly doing.

At the time, I thought I was just doing whatever it took to be successful. I thought I had to grind it out and work incredibly hard, in order to get anywhere in life, which was something I had witnessed and been told my whole life. It was not until I started to connect with my body and what it wanted, and then honoring that above all else, that I was able to feel truly connected and in flow with life.

At that point, I went from working such ridiculous amounts and burning myself out to working in a way that truly lights my soul on fire. I went from dating men who did not serve me to waiting for and receiving my king. The importance of feminine energy and being in balance cannot be overlooked. We feel this call, this pull, this longing for a new way of life, because it is what our soul truly, truly desires.

The way to begin connecting to your feminine energy is to get into your body. A good place to start is understanding and embracing the power of your menstrual cycle.

Women are naturally cyclical beings, as evidenced by our menstruation. Even if you are not currently menstruating, you still go through a cycle of hormones throughout a typical twenty-eight to thirty-five-day cycle. Throughout the month, our body goes through different phases that will bring about different needs and also abilities. Connecting to your natural cycle and beginning to embrace its power is one of the best ways to truly connect to your feminine core.

As someone who spent ten years on hormonal birth control and then was diagnosed with PCOS (polycystic ovarian syndrome), it was a process for me to get back to a place of balance within my body and then to love and appreciate my cycle.

I truly feel that learning to honor my body in each different stage has allowed me to connect to a deeper spirituality, to be more in tune with my desires and needs, and to feel more at peace with myself and my womanhood.

There is also even more power in embracing this part of womanhood because society holds so much shame and judgment around it. Once upon a time, I also held a great deal of shame and resentment toward my cycle. I had been conditioned, like many of us, that my bleeding was gross, even disgusting. I remember waking up to some blood on a boyfriend's bed and being absolutely mortified, then running quickly into the bathroom and getting a cloth to wipe it clean, before he could see it.

Think about all of the feminine care products you see in the grocery aisle. The scented tampons, the feminine wipes, and the washes. We are told by society our periods are something to hide. I am sure I'm not the only woman who has ever bled through her pants and been overcome with shame, hoping no one saw it. Or been filled with embarrassment that I had to ask my friend for a tampon, which are made in sleek packages to avoid detection—and for what? Have you ever thought to wonder why we would hold so much shame around something so natural and beautiful?

I now think of my monthly bleed as a welcome gift. But just a few years ago, I saw it as anything but. Like many women, I did not love or appreciate bleeding. I would often wonder why it is that women have to bleed and men have it so much easier. I saw it as an inconvenience and something I wished was not happening.

By reconnecting to this within myself, I have been able to tap into a deep love and appreciation for myself, my body, and my womanhood. And since I see this bleeding as a gift, it is now a welcome release of whatever is no longer serving me in my life.

Let's go into detail now about the power of your cycle and how to use it.

THE POWER OF YOUR CYCLE

I bleed every month
but do not die.
How am I not magic?

~Nayyirah Waheed

When I first learned about the power of our cycles, I was shocked. Why had no one told me about this? Why was this not taught in school? Why doesn't every woman on the planet know this?

Instead, we are told we are "crazy." We are ridiculed about "being on the rag," and many women even wear PMS like some kind of badge of honor, when, really, it is just a call from the body for your attention.

Every phase of your cycle has different strengths and signals. When you can sync up your lifestyle with these phases, you are in for a world of change. Your cycle can guide you in your creative projects, in your diet and exercise regime, and so much more!

It is important to note, getting back to your cyclical nature will be a total shift. It goes against so much of what you have been taught. Perhaps you are once like I was, obsessed with meal prepping, following a particular workout routine for no particular reason, or otherwise disconnected from ever asking your body what it actually needs. Getting in touch with your body and your cycle will be a life changing experience. It requires that you build a relationship of trust with yourself. It requires that you listen to your body and your intuition over what you "think" you should do.

To break it down in simple terms, you can think of your monthly cycle like the seasons.

Starting with days 0-7, while you are bleeding, this is *winter*. Think of winter in the typical sense, as a time when it is cold, the trees are barren, and you are more likely to want to stay inside and not be social. I regularly plan my schedule to have the entire first and second days of my cycle as total rest and relaxation. I turn the world off, and I tune in and release what is no longer serving me in my life.

This is a time when you are highly intuitive and considered to be closer to source. It is powerful to spend this time in reflection, tuning in to yourself and your body. This is the time to ask yourself for the answers you may be looking for. Perhaps you have a decision that is weighing on you. Go into meditation, and simply ask for the answer. *FEEL* the response in your womb, and trust it.

Your bleed is a truly powerful gift you've been given. When treated that way, it will change your relationship with yourself and your body forever.

Women in ancient cultures were known to be more powerful and wise when they were bleeding, and this was traditionally honored as a sacred time. Do you treat yourself and your body as sacred during this time? What can you do to honor yourself during your bleed?

When you use this time for clarity, it can set you up powerfully for the rest of your cycle. Perhaps you will get the intuitive download of your next steps, of what you need to do or create.

I encourage you to celebrate this time. I encourage you to make friends and peace with your period. Honor your body. Slow down, if you can. Give yourself permission to rest and just be. Skip the gym, and go for a walk out in nature, instead. Eat nourishing warming foods, wear red, and embrace your magic!

Perhaps you want to experiment with doing your own blood ritual. This is a powerful practice in reclamation of your womanhood. I highly suggest using a menstrual cup to collect your blood. You can keep a jar of it and use it then to make an intuitive painting or maybe even do your own "vampire facial" by using your blood as a face mask. Give it to your plants as a monthly fertilizer, and think of it as giving a gift back to the Earth, who gives you so much every single day.

If the idea of this triggers you or makes you cringe, that is okay. The conditioning runs deep. I first heard of doing blood rituals years before I ever did it myself. I remember thinking that the woman telling me about giving the Earth her blood was totally crazy! And who knows, maybe it *is* crazy. All I know is I have never felt more connected to myself, to my body, and to this planet we call home than I do after doing this work. And, as someone who likes to push the crazy envelope, I have taken my own blood-ritual practice even further.

I am slightly hesitant to admit this, as it is something very far from the mainstream, but from time to time, I also drink it. I had heard about this ancient tradition long before I tried it myself, and I was never planning to actually do it. In truth, the first time I heard about it, I thought it sounded disgusting *Why would I ever do that?!*

And what changed my mind? Intuition.

I have a rule: I always follow my intuition, and I do it quickly.

So, there I was, sitting on the toilet, having just pulled out my menstrual cup. Before pouring the contents into a jar, I heard that little whisper from within: *Drink this.*

Now, of course, I balked at the thought. "No, thank you!" I said. Then, just as I was about to pour it into the jar, I heard it even louder. *Drink this*!

Okay, I could not deny my body was asking me for this. So, I held the cup in my hand and brought it to my nose, just to check it out. To my surprise, it smelled wonderful, nourishing, and loving!

Without another thought, I said a little blessing, tilted my head back, and threw it down. I felt the power running through my veins as it slid down my throat. It felt like reclamation. It felt like defiance. And I loved every second of it.

I have now made this a regular practice, whenever I get the intuitive hit to do so. Our bodies are so intelligent, they will tell us exactly what they need. If you feel the pull and your flow is healthy, it might be something for you to try, too. If the mere thought makes you uneasy, then don't do it. Only you know what is best for you. I am just here to expand your mind and help you drop the shame about one of womanhood's greatest gifts.

The second phase is the *follicular phase*. As the seasons change, we can think of this time as spring. Just as the Earth begins to bloom then, your body is now building back up the lining of your uterus. Think of the things you might like to do in a typical spring. It feels new, fresh, and invigorating. So, this is a great time to try new activities. Maybe try a new workout class or go to that meetup you have been putting off. It is a great time to build a plan behind any of the intuitive ideas you may have gotten while you were bleeding. Tune into your body, and ask what it needs to eat. Perhaps your food choices are a little bit lighter during this time and include more fruits and vegetables.

The third phase is *ovulation*. Your monthly summer. Now is the time for a full social schedule, and when you may be able to work those long hours. You may be motivated to be in the gym more and do more intense activities. This is a great time to do some high-intensity cardio or that spin class you have been holding off on. This is the time to put that plan into action, to show up loudly and proudly. Ovulation makes you naturally magnetic, and you typically (although everyone is different) will feel the most energized and motivated. This is the time to answer your call and commit to what you are birthing into the world!

In this phase, I find I can work for long hours and still want to do more. I feel on fire and alive. I am also less hungry. Rather than prescribing to the typical dietary advice of eating three meals a day or however many calories, I honor my body's wishes, and I eat less.

The fourth phase is the *luteal phase* or fall. This is the time when, if the egg was not implanted during ovulation, your uterus will start getting the signals to shed, just like the Earth when leaves begin to fall.

Fall is one of my personal favorite seasons. This is a time to start to turn inward, a time when you may be asking yourself what needs to shed, and a time to dive into yourself and speak your truth. This is a time to embrace your inner Wild Woman. There is a certain sense of ruthlessness in this phase, including the ability to see through inauthenticity and not be afraid to speak on it. It is a time to set your boundaries and get focused on what needs to go and ensuring what is serving you will stay. With this refocusing, you are able to create powerful work. I often find, during this time in my cycle, I just don't give AF. I say what I want to say, I do what I want to do, and I just let it feel good. I also notice I am much hungrier in my luteal phase. I crave potatoes and other filling, warm foods. I allow myself to eat the extra food without any attachment to it.

Of course, these revelations were not given to me overnight. The only way to connect with this aspect of yourself is to track it. Keep a journal by your bed. Keep track of how you are feeling. Start to notice your patterns. When you are hungry, eat. When you are tired, rest. We are not meant to be "on" all of the time. The more attuned you become to this aspect of yourself, the more embodied and powerful you will be.

By being in tune with your cycle and getting accustomed to listening to what your body needs and wants, you are already doing so much work to be in your feminine energy and embodiment. You will feel more connected to yourself and your intuition.

Intuition lives in the body. The answers you seek are in the body, not in the head, and yet this is where you constantly go to make decisions. You are thinking your way through life. The feminine is not logical, and she is not linear. Start your day off by asking your body what it needs. Get accustomed to feeling instead of thinking. Being in this energy will allow you to tap into a greater power, your connection to source, and to make changes at a rapid pace.

And now, we will explore deepening this connection to your body through sexuality.

RECONNECT AND RECLAIM YOUR SEXUALITY

Can you taste the divinity on your lips?
Do you see it in your thighs, your hips?
Woman, you are magnificent.
Perfect in your presence.
A manifestation of the divine.
Your body is sacred.
Your power unmatched.
Embody it now, it is time.

~Kelly Kristin

To be in your feminine energy is to be sensual, tuned in, and turned on. Unfortunately, sexual shame runs deep in our society. We live in a world where women are simultaneously praised for baring it all and called whores and sluts for doing so. Add in religious views that shun sex before marriage and renounce the concept of pleasure, and I mean *really*! How could you not be confused?

It doesn't just stop there. We are constantly bombarded with sexuality in masculine nature, from pornography showcasing only men's desire and viewpoints to movies idolizing the traditional role of men overpowering women. We are also told that men are more sexual and there is some biological difference making men desire more than women. A woman who expresses a lot of sexual desire is subsequently shamed for being a slut.

Here is what you need to know. Sexual desire is normal and natural. There is nothing shameful or wrong about it. Your sexual energy is the energy of creation, and when you learn to tap into this aspect of yourself, you become more and more powerful. Tapping into this sexual energy does not mean you have to have sex with a lot of people or even desire to. It is about learning to find pleasure in all ways and increasing the life-force energy that flows through you.

In our current society, experiencing pleasure is a rebellious act. It requires you to slow down, to be present, and to throw out a lot of the constructs and beliefs you may have grown up with.

Let me assure you, you would not have been gifted with a clitoris if you were not supposed to experience pleasure. There are more nerve endings in your clitoris than any other part of any human body. I told you women are magic!

Like most women, I struggled with my own sexual expression. I was afraid of being "too much." I was afraid of being called a slut. I held a lot of shame around my first sexual experiences and even within my relationships. Reconnecting back to the truth of what I desired sexually required release of this shame.

The first time I decided to release my sexual shame, I asked my unconscious mind when I had first experienced this. To my surprise, I was taken back many lifetimes ago and shown an image of me as an African boy. I was naked in the village, playing around with girls. I began to stroke my penis and my mother came out and started to yell at me. I instantly felt the shame; it was so profound. I asked my unconscious what it needed to learn, to be able to release this.

What was the message?

I was just a child. It was natural. It felt good, and there was nothing wrong with it. Children explore.

The feeling of shame instantly lifted out of my body.

Upon my journey back to the moment of now, I felt the times when this had affected me throughout my personal history. I felt the shame around "losing my virginity" just gone, and the times when I was in less-than-desirable sexual circumstances. It was all lifted and dissolved in just a few minutes. Then, I was back in my body with a new level of understanding and a need to explore.

Being a woman in my late twenties at that time, I realized I had never really learned anything about sex. (Most of us never actually do.) It is one of those things we think we should just automatically know how to do, and so we devote little to no time studying it or enhancing our skills. I wanted to change this, so I began studying tantra and womb healing. I began cultivating my own sexual energy through touch, breath, and meditation.

For the first time in my life, I learned how to pleasure myself for the sake of pleasure. How to treat myself like the queen I am, in the bedroom and beyond. I took on lovers purely for pleasure, with no guilt. I allowed myself to be louder and surrender to the moment. I decided it was all about me, that my pleasure was going to come first (no pun intended). I decided to be more playful and free. I became a student of pleasure, a practice I am still learning and growing with.

Sexual energy is healing. It is creation. It is life. And it just may be the missing piece on your empowerment journey.

It is time to drop the guilt and shame around your sexuality and accept yourself as you are. This is a conscious choice to make. You can choose now to wipe the slate clean and accept who and what you are and desire. What if your desires are not wrong or right? What if they just *are*?

Take, for instance, my client, Lucy. She took one of my sexual empowerment courses. She had been feeling a disconnection from herself and her body. She had desires she didn't know how to express in her marriage. Having grown up in the Catholic Church, she also felt incredibly guilty for having them.

As we worked to release the stories around sexuality and the shame she felt for wanting something different, along with the emotions from the past, she became more and more comfortable with her truth. She desired multiple partners within her marriage. She wanted to explore her sexuality with women and other couples. After breaking through and having this conversation with her husband, she now happily reports a highly satisfying sex life and a deeper bond with her husband.

There is no right or wrong way to live your life, as long as you are not hurting anyone else in the process.

Being able to express yourself sensually and sexually is truly the domain of a woman in her feminine power. This energy carries over into everything you do. Learning to speak up and express desires in the bedroom has a direct effect on how you show up and express yourself in your life. This is a vital process for any woman who wants to speak her truth.

If there was no such thing as shame, if shame did not exist, if you could not be wrong or bad for desiring anything, then what? What do you desire?

Reclaiming your sexuality is, of course, not only about sex. It is about living your life in a sensual and turned-on way. What if everything around you could be pleasurable and joyful?

When was the last time you ate for pleasure, enjoying every bite of it, and letting the juiciness of a strawberry delight your senses as you pierced its skin with your teeth?

When was the last time you walked by the mirror, touched yourself, and said, "Damn, I look good!"

When was the last time you took a bath and caressed and loved on every part of your body?

This is all connected. The more you can do the above, the more sexual energy you will cultivate, leading to more confidence in the bedroom and beyond. The more turned on you are, the more in tune you are with your body and your intuition.

Think about it. I already told you there is a direct link between your uterus and your brain. Your sexual energy begins in the womb, and the womb is where your intuition lies. As you expand your capacity of sexual energy, you are creating more awareness in your womb space and thus increasing your intuitive capabilities.

I want you to practice feeling into your intuition for a moment.

Think about a situation in the past when you had to make a decision, when you were going back and forth about what to do.

Go back to that time now, and float down into your body. See what you saw, hear what you heard, and feel what you felt. In your body, do you feel expansion or contraction?

Expansion is a *yes*. Contraction is a *no*. Practice this now, as you move forward in your life. Ask yourself questions, and *feel* the answer in your body.

The answer may not always seem "logical," but that is precisely the point. The feminine is not logical. It is your choice to trust yourself enough to follow your nudges.

The more connected you are to your body, the easier it will be to trust yourself and your intuition. I recommend you develop a daily practice of getting into your body. My favorite ways to connect to my body are touch, breath, and movement. These things ground me and allow me to cultivate my sensual life-force energy.

Breath is the easiest and can be done anytime, anywhere. If you are in a heightened state or are feeling disconnected, breathe. Concentrate your energy to your womb space and just breathe. When you wake up in the morning, breathe intentionally. Feel the breath in your body. Then, caress your skin; touch and feel every part of yourself.

Have a daily practice of intentional movement. Put on some sultry music, and swing those hips! Feel the energy ignited in your womb space. Take it even further by doing a pole dance class or something that takes you out of your sensual comfort zone.

Being a woman is so fun and magical. It is time to start living into it and experiencing it. Your body is meant to be a source of pleasure and bliss, not something you are constantly trying to change or wish was different.

The more you love your body and find joy and pleasure in each and every moment, the more you will radiate your natural magnetism. And that is a super power all on its own!

THE EMPOWERED FEMININE

Of course, like with all things, the goal here is not to be in your feminine energy 100% of the time, it is a spectrum, and going too far into the feminine is not ideal.

This call for reconnection is also a call for awareness of how you show up as a woman in this world. The women who are purely or mostly in their feminine energy can seem floaty and ungrounded or weak, unable to bring goals and visions into reality. This may be a woman who is in an endless healing cycle, with little action and integration. It could be someone who is obsessed with the inner work and not moving forward. This could be a woman who knows she has so much to give to the world and is a natural-born leader, yet she falls victim to the fear instead of answering the call.

The goal is to have a balance of masculine and feminine energy. When in balance, you are in tune with yourself, your body, your intuition, and your desires, and you act on those things. You are radiant and magnetic. You utilize your gifts and connection with source to show up as a powerful woman in this world.

I would also be remiss if I did not mention the difference between being in your empowered feminine and being in a wounded feminine state. So much of the collective is rooted in a wounded feminine state. This is, of course, perpetuated by the patriarchy and societal standards of what is beautiful.

The wounded feminine manifests as a woman who is obsessed with looks and dreads the idea of getting older. She may present as a "girly-girl" with a deep-seated fear of being seen without being completely made up. The woman feels competitive toward other women, because she has bought into the lies that society perpetuates that there is not enough to go around. She sees another woman's beauty as a threat.

Her validation and worth are tied into others' perceptions. She is so concerned with the judgment of others because she judges herself so harshly. She lacks true love and acceptance for herself as herself. She feels disconnected from herself and her inner power, although she may not even be aware of it. She is waiting on a man or someone else to come save her in her life. She often attracts relationships that are toxic and co-dependent.

It is no wonder so many women are in this wounded state. It is what our modern patriarchal society programs us to be. Sisterhood wounding is deep. We are constantly pitted against one another in television and movies. We are told women are "catty" and can't be trusted.

I am sure you can think of a circumstance in your life where you were betrayed on some level by a woman whom you thought was your friend or even a family member who reinforced that belief.

THE CALL TO RISE

Society tells us we are not allowed to get wrinkles, through marketing anti-aging and Botox injections to those in their twenties. We are shown PhotoShopped images in magazines and idolize celebrities who have had massive amounts of plastic surgery. The truth being you could not look like that person unless you paid to.

I will never forget going to a plastic surgeon's office to get under-eye fillers. (Yes, I, too, can buy into the lies.) I was told I also needed Botox. I said repeatedly I did not want it and was fine with how I looked.

This doctor proceeded to go through every section of my face, telling me I would need surgery soon, if I did not start with the Botox now.

I was appalled, offended, and, at the same time, grateful I had done the work on my own self-worth, so I could ignore these comments and hold to myself. I never went back to that office, nor have I gotten filler since. Instead, I dove deeper into loving myself and caring for myself in soul-nourishing ways. This single experience allowed me to rise further into my empowerment.

Upon leaving that office, I really decided to question my motives. Was I there because I really needed the under-eye filler? Why did I not feel beautiful without it? Was this really *my* choice?

I am not here to judge anyone else for what they do or don't do to their face or body. I still get facials, get my hair done, dress up, and wear makeup. I just no longer do these things to please anyone else or try to fit myself into some ridiculous standard. I spent most of my life in a wounded state. I never left the house without makeup. I was obsessed with dieting and going to the gym to lose weight. I didn't trust other women easily and was constantly judging them based on their looks, what they wore, or how they were acting.

Now, I get dressed up when I choose to express myself in that way. I wear makeup when I choose to express myself in that way. I no longer feel like I must look a certain way to be accepted. I accept other women as they are. I don't judge them. I love them. I believe in sisterhood and the good of others.

This doesn't mean I have to like every woman I meet. It means I let her do her and I do me. Being empowered instead of wounded has led me to freedom to just be me.

Awareness of how you are showing up as a woman and how you treat other women is imperative to your self-growth. This is not about blaming or shaming yourself for potentially being in a wounded state. This is simply your *call to rise*.

This is your call to rise up and be the empowered woman you know you are. To join in true sisterhood. To love yourself deeply and accept yourself fully.

The patriarchal society has oppressed women because we are powerful. There would be no need for oppression, if this were not true. When we do the work to break these constructs and live in an empowered feminine state, we are changing the world.

The empowered woman is a danger to society as it currently is, because she doesn't follow the rules. She doesn't buy into the lies about not being enough. She marches to the beat of her own drum, and she lives without concern of judgment.

The woman in her empowered feminine embraces her natural beauty and uniqueness. She knows she is worthy just as she is. She knows she is enough. Worth does not come from looks, from how much money is in her bank account, or from what she does for a living. Worth is inherent.

Her focus is on collaboration, and she works to help other women rise as she has. She radiates divine love and wholeness, and she attracts co-creative and healthy relationships. She is only willing to take on a partner who can meet her where she is at and enhance her life.

She is in love with herself and life. She knows herself to be an aspect of the divine. She is connected to source power and knows she is supported by the entire Universe. This connection leads her to feel safe and trusting in her own inner power.

The importance of this connection to source power cannot be overlooked. Call it God, call it the Universe, angels—whatever feels good to you and allows you to tap into a connection that is beyond physical human form.

When you can trust in this support system, you can be in your feminine magic. You know you are always being held, guided, and directed.

Allow yourself to feel supported right now. Take a slow deep breath and hold it in. Feel the air fill you, and become aware of the sensations in your body. If you are sitting, feel whatever is underneath you, and literally allow yourself to feel the support beneath your feet. Go outside and connect to nature. Go where you feel best. For me, the ocean has always called to me. It is a place where I always seem to be able to tap in further and feel the connection beyond me. You are always being supported. Lean into that support when you need to.

Part of being empowered is surrender. Yes, that is quite the paradox! I do not mean surrender in a way of giving up. I mean surrender in a way of surrendering to a power greater than you in human form. Surrender in the form of asking for guidance from your connection to source. Being aware now of what your desires are, allow this connection to guide you about how to attain them. When you are open to the guidance, it will come.

Think of yourself now. Are you more wounded or are you empowered? In what areas do you need to love and accept yourself? In what ways do you need to heal the sisterhood wound? Where do you need to drop your judgments and replace them with love? Do you have a spiritual connection practice?

Perhaps you need to do a social-media detox. Delete any and all accounts you follow that cause you to question your beauty or worth. Clean up your friend circle, and associate with other women who feel the call to rise, too. Get out of your comfort zone, and join in on a local women's circle. Be a woman you would want to befriend.

REPROGRAM

You now know how to connect to yourself, to your intuition, and your desires.

Now it is time to reprogram your mind and body to be the person who is able to receive it.

This part of the process is *essential* to truly living your life in a new way. Most people try to change themselves by being the same person they always were. But, in order for you to truly live a new life, to have the things you have never had before, and to do the things you have never done before, you must be someone whom you have never been before.

Now, by releasing, by having a deep and true connection to yourself, you are certainly on the way to being a new person. However, if you do not install a new program (a belief, value, identity, or story), the only option will be to go back to the old one. That is why so many people can move forward and feel like they are making progress and change, yet they fall back into their old ways time and time again.

There is nothing special about the people whom you think have it all—the money, the relationships, the business, the joy, and happiness. They are simply running different programs, and this is all available to you.

It is important to note, while you may start thinking, "Oh my, I have so much releasing to do before I can reprogram," that simply isn't true. Because we have released negative emotions from the root cause, you will fundamentally and genetically be a different person and already available for new ways of being. It is not necessary to go back through every limiting belief before you begin to reprogram, and it would not even be possible. As you continue to grow and expand, you will have new levels, new understandings, and new limitations you didn't even know were there. It is not a cause for worry.

Rather than looking for limiting beliefs that you need to get rid of, we can program your mind and body to feel safe to experience the things you desire.

As I explained earlier, the number-one thing your subconscious mind does is keep you safe. It is actually of no use to program beliefs into your mind unless your subconscious *feels* safe to experience it. This is why affirmations are not very effective. Sure, they can be a good starting point and help you think more positively. They just don't really do what you think they do.

Imagine you are wanting more confidence, something many of my clients desire. And every morning you look at yourself in the mirror and repeat the affirmation, "I am confident." Yet you feel insecure. Maybe you are looking at yourself in judgment and not loving what you see in the mirror.

And then again, later in the day, you are going into a meeting and want to be confident, so you repeat the affirmation, "I am confident." Yet you feel insecure, questioning your expertise and hoping nothing goes wrong.

Your subconscious mind has no idea what the words "I am confident" even mean. In the above scenario, you might even be doing more harm than good as you are creating a neural network that links feeling insecure with the word "confident." The subconscious interprets based in sight, sound, and feeling.

If you want to be confident, you must ask yourself, "What are you seeing, hearing, and feeling?" when you *already* are confident and can get your mind and body into that scenario. Quite literally, what is the vision or picture that comes to your mind when you think "I am confident"?

Perhaps you see yourself dancing in the mirror. Maybe you see yourself absolutely excelling at a presentation and you receive praise from your boss. Once you define that, close your eyes, and allow the feeling to arise within you. Hold on to it for as long as you can, as often as you can. This is how you recondition your mind and body to experience a new reality. Additionally, you can recall a past time when you felt confident. Again, float down into your body, see what you saw, hear what you heard, and feel what you felt. Then you can correctly affirm, "I am confident!"

Feeling is creating a vibration and energy within you that will quite literally pull closer to you that which you desire in the quantum field. If you get nothing else out of this book and any of my teachings besides the understanding that emotions and feelings are what actually create your reality, then I have done my job.

Emotions are energy, and energy creates a vibrational frequency. This frequency is information you are sending out into the universe. The more time you can experience high-vibration emotions such as gratitude, love, and joy, the better your life and your experience of reality will be. Now, while feeling these emotions will undoubtedly bring about change, when you attach these high-vibration emotions with the vision for your future, magic happens.

When you are grateful for what you wish to experience before you actually do and feel the feelings of having it already, you will soon not have to imagine it anymore. It will become your reality.

In my understanding and use of the quantum-reality model, there is no time and no space. There is only the moment of now, and everything is occurring right now in the field of pure potentiality. In actuality, you already have the things you desire. The desires in your heart, the images you see, the vision you have for yourself are all there because you are experiencing it in a parallel universe. You would not desire it if you were not already experiencing it in the quantum. And the way to pull it in to your existence so you may experience it in this reality is to vibrationally align with it. Feel the feelings of already having it.

In short, imagine how it would feel to already have the thing you desire. Get a clear picture in your mind. What do you see? What do you hear? What do you feel? Allow the feelings to arise through your body. Go to that place as often as you can.

The truth is our unconscious mind can-not tell the difference between what you are seeing with your eyes open or imagining in your mind with eyes closed. If what you are doing when your eyes are closed begins to feel more real than your everyday life walking around, you are going to make massive changes in your life.

Now, of course, if you do this for twenty minutes a day and the other twenty-three hours and forty minutes are spent with feelings, thoughts, and beliefs that are *not* in alignment with your vision, it will not be able to make manifest. So, you must dig a little deeper.

To become the powerful woman you are meant to be, you must first decide what that empowerment looks like. What makes me feel powerful and alive and joyous is, most likely, different for you. We are all unique, with our own desires we have been given and visions that we have.

When you are the most empowered version of yourself, when you are living life as the powerful woman you know you are destined to be, what does your life look like?

When you envision yourself and your life as this empowered version of yourself, what are your beliefs, thoughts, and daily actions?

For example, if you desire to experience a financially abundant life, what would a person who is financially abundant believe? Would they believe that making money is easy or hard? Would they talk about how difficult it is to make money all day long? Would they hold onto every dollar they got for dear life? Or would they understand that money is a renewable resource?

Your beliefs, thoughts, and actions should be reflective of your vision, not your current reality. Do not be fooled by the simplicity of this process. You have been thinking and being a different way for a very long time, and this change will be uncomfortable. It is often easier to forget and go back to old ways of being. While visualizing can and will create a new neural pathway, you always have a choice to take it or not.

Think about it like this. You are going for a hike you have taken every day for the last twenty years. The trail is clear, there is no resistance, and you know when the next turn is. You could practically walk it with your eyes closed. The destination is nothing special.

One day, you hear there is a beautiful waterfall hidden in the woods, and you decide you want to go and find it. You hike a different way, thus creating a new path. This new path requires you to move some bushes out of the way. The terrain is rugged with many rocks, and the grass is higher than you thought it would be.

You start to doubt whether you are going the right direction. You are not sure how to get to the destination. You think, maybe it would just be easier to take the old path, so you give up and go back to the old path.

The next day, you go for your hike again. You see the faint new trail and try again. You still feel unsure, yet you continue to walk in faith, believing you will get there. And alas, you do! The waterfall is even more beautiful than you imagined!

The next day, you go on the hike again. You see the split in the path of the old way, and you can still barely see where you started the new trail. You feel reluctance and know it would be so much easier to take the clear, known path. Yet you are determined to create this path and overcome this challenge, to get to this waterfall. You continue to push the discomfort and take the new path again and again. Over time, this path becomes more and more clear. Each time you take this path, it becomes easier. Of course, the old path is still there and available for you to take. It is a *choice* to take this new path.

Your mind is the same way. You can actually create a new neural pathway in a matter of minutes, especially when utilizing modalities that incorporate energy psychology. I am a facilitator and a huge advocate for PSYCH-K®. This is a process that utilizes the brain and body connection to form new neural pathways within minutes.

Alternately, you can continue to visualize and feel the feelings of already having the thing that you desire. This, depending on how "far-fetched" it feels to your subconscious and the state of your nervous system, can take a while to take hold. If you continue to work at it, the connection will happen, and you will then be able to choose that new pathway over and over again to solidify it.

And while this energy talk and visualization can seem woo-woo, please know it is heavily rooted in neuropsychology. In its simplest form, this is based on the idea that neurons that fire together wire together. You want to be sure you are linking positive, high-vibration emotions with the vision.

Beyond meditating and visualizing, the work comes in constantly making the choice to shift. This requires presence. This requires being aware of the thoughts you are thinking and the feelings you are feeling. As you become aware, you are making the unconscious conscious. You are separating yourself from the thought and feeling by observing the thought or feeling.

This simple act makes a tremendous difference, because it actually signals to your nervous system to relax where it could otherwise be triggered. By bringing awareness to it, you are able to shift it to what you would like to feel or think. The more you do this shifting, the easier it will become. It is so simple and yet something we so often forget. You have choice. If you want to stop suffering, if you want to stop feeling a certain way, choose the new path.

If you find yourself in a negative thought or feeling, it is not about resisting the feeling. Allow yourself to feel it, and then be done with it. Feel the feeling, and then choose a new thought.

To ease integration in your life, there are some tools you can use. One that can be immensely powerful is to record yourself speaking your vision clearly, stating what you see, hear, and feel. This is a form of self-hypnosis. You can also use this to program in the new beliefs and actions you need to take, in order to see your vision come to fruition. You can simply record yourself on your phone and listen to it as you fall asleep at night. This is a time when the subconscious becomes more open to suggestion.

The morning is also a powerful time to work with your mind. Start your day off by first tuning into your body. Touch yourself and say hello. Say beautiful things to yourself as you look in the mirror and start your day on a positive note, before you pick up the phone and get to scrolling.

Beyond that, working with a practitioner who truly understands how to tap into the power of the subconscious mind is invaluable. I have seen clients start a singular session and go from lost, crying, and feeling unworthy to feeling better about themselves and their lives than ever before.

Take, for instance, my client Ashley. She came to me for a Rapid Transformation Session. She was feeling lost, like she could not be her true self around people. She wanted so badly to feel freedom within herself and her body and the freedom to express her true self.

In the session, we released the idea that she was not safe to be herself. She reconnected to her vision of what it would actually look, feel, and sound like to live life in full expression. Then, we did a Psych-K$^{\circledR}$ balance, to program that in.

A couple of months later, I spoke to Ashley, and she told me that the *exact* vision we had programmed in had happened! She was sitting around a campfire, singing songs with friends—something she had never felt comfortable doing before. Together, we had created the pathway, and when presented with the choice, she took it.

It never ceases to blow my mind just how profound and life-changing this work can be.

RECONDITIONING THE BODY

As you have most likely gathered, the body plays an invaluable role in our experience of reality. Yes, we are cosmic beings with limitless potential. And we are also on this Earth now, having a human experience inside of a human body. This means we have a nervous system that needs to be regulated.

Our nervous system shares the duty, with our subconscious mind, of keeping us safe. Remember, the mind signals the body; that is how we feel emotions like fear. While your release of these emotions and your trauma from their root cause will have profound effects, it does not mean you are never going to experience them again.

You will, at times, still feel fear. Most of the time, however, this fear is unwarranted; it is just a reaction to how we have evolved as a species. Fear is there to protect you. If you are walking in the street and hear gunshots, you feel fear and go run for cover. This is an appropriate response to the fear, and your nervous system is doing its job to protect you.

More often than not, in modern society, the fear you feel is not tied to a life-threatening situation that your body is signaling to you. You may also feel the same fear when you choose to undertake some new endeavors in life.

I remember the time I held my first public women's circle. The butterflies were flying in my stomach! I doubted myself and my readiness, and I tried to talk myself out of it so many times. But I felt the fear and did it anyway. Now, I still feel butterflies, but it is more like excitement than fear, because I know how fun and transformational the events are.

In a similar way, I was terrified the first time I put out a public program. I had so many thoughts running through my head: What if no one buys it? What if it isn't good enough? Again, I did it anyway. I continue to face and push through new fears daily.

You must do the things you are terrified to do. Just as taking a new path is about creating a new pathway in your mind, so is it also about creating a new reaction in your body. Fear can no longer be an excuse. You can train your body to be okay doing the things you fear by doing the things you fear. Once you do what you fear, your body knows it is safe to do it, and each time you go to do it, the reaction will become less and less.

Once you know the rapid transformation process and you can release from the root cause, your process will undoubtedly be easier. Yet you still have the choice to follow the old path or the new path.

As a woman in today's society, we must do particular work to recondition our body for new experiences. We are in a new paradigm for women. We are taking on more and more leadership roles and reclaiming our power as healers and wise women. We are now free to choose!

The fear of being seen and heard will come up. Every time you feel the fear, lean in, find your edge, and push past it. If you are afraid to speak in public, *speak*. If you are afraid to be seen, wear something bold and colorful. Take up space!

Yes, it will be uncomfortable. However, that is exactly where the growth is. Allow yourself to grow through each and every experience. As you continue to push past your limitations, remind yourself you are worthy and it is safe to experience all that you desire.

In meditation, practice seeing, hearing, and feeling the feelings of having what you desire. Practice holding the feeling and the energy and letting it expand throughout your body. Feel the feelings of having what you desire over and over again until it shows up in your life.

THE RAPID TRANSFORMATION PROCESS IN YOUR LIFE

Just like moons and like suns,
With the certainty of tides,
Just like hopes springing high,
Still I'll rise.

~ Maya Angelou

This is not just meant to be a book you read and forget about.

No, sister. This is *your* call to rise.

You are the master of your own universe. If nothing else, I want you to understand that you are responsible for creating your life. No matter where you are, no matter what you have gone through, you can rise, and you *will*, if you choose to.

Reality is largely an illusion, and you are capable of changing it. The rapid transformation process is intended for use in any area of your life you are less than satisfied with.

I have laid out the steps for you to be able to transform your life from the inside out and live in a new way. How you choose to integrate and utilize this information is up to you.

You must first decide. You must decide you are not only capable of healing and becoming the powerful woman you are meant to be, but it is your destiny.

I find myself constantly wondering what will happen when we women finally get it together. When we finally realize our power, our *divine* feminine power, that exists within all of us. I imagine a time and place where we all uplift one another. When we fight for one another not *with* one another. A time when we all radiate love and wholeness. A time when we all embrace our womanhood and everything that comes along with it.

THE CALL TO RISE

I won't tell you that awakening and reclaiming your power is easy. Doing this work may be the most difficult thing you ever do in your life. It was for me. And there are still times when it is hard.

There are times when I still have to remind myself not to shrink because I think other people won't get it or won't like me. I have to remind myself that this calling is beyond me. Every time I share with another woman a piece of myself that I was once ashamed of or that I hid away, I am reminded why I do this. This isn't *for* me or *about* me at all.

I am here for you. I am here to see you, to hear you, and to witness your pain, so you may be free of it.

I'm here to show you how to step into and embrace your power, so you can shine the light that's within you.

I hope you know how magical and powerful you truly are. This level of empowerment, peace, and self-love is available for you as soon as you are willing to let go of all your reasons why it isn't.

No more hiding.

No more playing small.

No more waiting.

You are worthy right now.

You are capable right now.

It is time to be the powerful woman you came here to be.

It is time to live your life in your full expression.

This is your call to rise.

Will you answer it?

I want to thank you for taking this journey with me. For reading this book and hopefully integrating these principles and practices in your life.

As a special gift for reading the book, I would love to send you a powerful meditation designed to expand your energetic capacity to stand in your power. Please email me at kellykristincoaching@gmail.com to request it.

If you are interested in experiencing this work first-hand, please email here for all my latest offerings: kellykristincoaching@gmail.com.

You can keep up with this conversation and much more by tuning into the Woman Unleashed Podcast.

ACKNOWLEDGMENTS

There have been so many powerful women who have come before me and paved this path. I want to acknowledge every woman who has healed herself and allowed me to heal. I acknowledge every woman for doing the work to make this world a safer place to rise. Thank you.

ABOUT KELLY

KELLY KRISTIN is a coach and mentor to women all over the world who are ready to connect and embody their innate feminine power. She specializes in working with the subconscious mind and divine feminine power to help her clients release and heal emotional trauma from the root, reconnect to their feminine energy, and reprogram their minds and body to live in a new reality.

KELLY KRISTIN

She is a registered nurse with a background in psychiatry and a certified holistic health coach. She is science and research junkie with an affinity for neuroscience and the mind-body connection. She is also an NLP practitioner, a *PSYCH-K*® facilitator, clinical hypnotherapist, and spiritual thought leader.

CPSIA information can be obtained
at www.ICGtesting.com
Printed in the USA
LVHW112312041119
636249LV00006B/512/P